# THE PARTING GLASS

## Poems

# THE PARTING GLASS

## Poems

Lisa J. Parker

## MADVILLE
PUBLISHING

LAKE DALLAS, TEXAS

*The Parting Glass* is the first winner of the annual Arthur Smith Poetry Prize, established in 2021 by Madville Publishing in honor and memory of Art's many years of teaching, mentoring, and fine poetics.

Grateful thanks to judge Jesse Graves and to readers David Kitchel, Curt Rode, and Linda Parsons—all former students of Art Smith.

Cover Photo: Lisa J. Parker
Cover Design: Brian Hurst
Author Photo: Laura Coleman

ISBN: 978-1-956440-16-4 paperback
978-1-956440-17-1 ebook
Library of Congress Control Number: 2022937358

*For Scott*

*For the unnamed fallen*

*And for my family, always my family,
especially my parents, Chuck and Sue Parker*


*In memory of Tracey Furr
(1971-2021)*

*and Linda Whitt Schubert
(1954-2019)*

# Contents

| | |
|---|---|
| 1 | Lessons on Trees |
| 2 | What We Kill to Save |
| 3 | Prevarication |
| 4 | Big K Radio: Snow Day |
| 6 | Ars Poetica: Northern Virginia |
| 7 | The Preacher's Daughter Studies Her Reflection |
| 8 | You Can't Leave It When You Go |
| 13 | Hillbilly Transplant: Starling in Gingko |
| 14 | Hillbilly Transplant: Seeing Child on Junction Boulevard Subway Platform |
| 15 | Hillbilly Transplant: Where I Live |
| 16 | Hillbilly Transplant Writes "Where I'm From" Exercise with Imposter Narrative |
| 17 | Hillbilly Transplant: New Home |
| 18 | Hillbilly Transplant: In 72nd Street Subway Tunnel a Meditation on Home |
| 20 | Hillbilly Transplant: Seed and Scatter |
| 22 | Hillbilly Transplant: Pondering Park Dominoes and the Death of Celia Cruz |
| 24 | Hillbilly Transplant: Working at the Metropolitan Opera |
| 26 | Contrapuntal: Driving as the Flood Comes |
| 29 | Benefaction |
| 31 | Under the Sugar Moon |
| 32 | Under the Flower Moon: What We Plant |
| 33 | Tracer |
| 34 | Heaving |
| 35 | Deployment: Homefront |
| 36 | At the VA |

37    Beautiful

39    Cleave

43    Zebras Through the Fire

45    Painting of Grief: Exhibit of Aztec Goddess at the Met

46    Hillbilly Transplant: Bethesda Fountain, Central Park

47    In Ithaca Reflecting on the Death of Poet Kathryn Stripling Byer

48    Hillbilly Transplant Finds No Frame of Reference

49    Thus Always to Tyrants

51    Hillbilly Transplant: Upper West Side, October 10, 2001

52    Smoke, Salt, Sweet

54    Observations of Escape

55    Memorial Day

56    [Us]

58    Solace: What Slips the Horizon

59    Pandemic Months

60    Pandemic Months: And Still All Around Us

62    Flash

63    Republic 2017-2020

64    Cannery in Seasons

69    Passing of Grief

70    What Becomes of Song


72    Publications

73    Acknowledgments

75    About the Author

Of all the money that e'er I had
I spent it in good company
And all the harm I've ever done
Alas it was to none but me
And all I've done for want of wit
To memory now I can't recall
So fill to me the parting glass
Good night and joy be to you all


*From the traditional Irish folk song
"The Parting Glass"*

# Lessons on Trees

I don't remember knowing how to knot the ropes
my father fashioned over my shoulder as a kid,
or if he said, *Be careful*
or pointed what limbs were best to hold me
once he'd hefted me in the tree, only the feel
of his shoulders under my feet, the way his hands
circled my calves whole when he pushed me higher.

Had you seen the yard that day we bore
the big tulip poplar down and away from the house,
you would've seen the tentative reach and pull
of a girl held by nothing but will
and her father standing, hands raised explaining
fulcrum and leverage, *bit higher, little more,*
*almost there, tie it off.*

Years later, home from the hospital, he stands
watching from the window as we heft his granddaughter
into the branches of a stubborn hickory can't keep
from leaning toward garden and house.
He watches how we run the pull rope around a pin oak,
taps the window pointing to a larger one a few feet away.

We manage the tree down with careful chainsaw wedges,
ropes, wide oak fulcrum, and his granddaughter halfway
across the yard when it falls. She waves a thumbs-up at us
from her perch on the split-rail and I wonder
what we cheated her in all our precautions,
what singular gratitude you might only realize when falling
and suddenly caught by branches or to hit the ground full force,
throat clutched with air knocked clean out of you and that first
sweet wheeze when diaphragm unlocks and shudders.

# What We Kill to Save

Today it's tree vine around hickory,
a decade of slow choke, beautiful metastasis,
it cripples its way up the bark,
so savage its grip that Dad's swing
can sever only top from bottom,
and sweat pocks his forehead
as he runs the axe blade over
and over against the mooring veins,
the tight weave anchored so deep
pieces of bark come away as he pulls,
leaving the meat scarred with lines
like hieroglyphics or hair splayed
against a pillow, and the vine dangles
a headless snake in his hands, oozing
slow droplets that smell like oak tussin
and our foreheads touch as we sniff the stump
like animals at a fresh kill,
and I surprise us both touching
the amputated piece to my tongue,
my mouth suddenly full of alfalfa-summer.
Dad straightens himself,
lets go the vine where it stands
recalcitrant in the ground, cleaved
by only a few inches from its top half,
both ends weeping a steady flow.
Mottled brown spring peepers move in
even before we've left, buzzards
to the carnage, their bodies shiny and covered
in the wet, loamy aftermath.

# Prevarication

At the edge of yard
I watched blackberry vines for readiness,
squeezed nascent buds as red to purple to black,
vines inching taller against their cling and twine around
silvery anchor cable on the telephone pole.

Mama warned of electrocution when she caught me
shimmying half its length toward a tangled kite, told me
my hands could be burned clear off, I might end up
in a wheelchair like her cousin Jimmy
who worked for Dominion Power
and got thrown 50 feet,
the imprint of his body
burned into the grass.

I wondered what wild thing could make a blackberry
stronger than a man, ran my fingers
against vines until they touched cable, pressed
my luck until I grabbed the whole thing in my fist, held
tighter with each passing minute until slowly the fallacy
of my mother's warning became clear
and I walked bowl after bowl of berries in to her,
never another thing mentioned,
even years later, the countless syrups and preserves
she spooned or spread over bread she pushed
into my mouth when I was too sick to feed myself,
her careful conservation the only thing that could sustain me.

# Big K Radio: Snow Day

*for Laura*

My sister wakes me to heavy snow, her small belly
in my face as she leans over me to pull back curtains
on the window above the bed. We squint sleep away,
stare at the strange gray of pre-dawn,
listen to the pelt against glass.
We drag Grandma's quilts downstairs, watch
the window for first dawn when we can wake
our folks without trouble. We carry the radio with us,
creep the knob through the static and crackle of AM stations:
Roger Miller sings, *I'm the seventh out of seven sons*
*my pappy's a pistol, I'm a son of a gun*, a commercial
for Broadview Auto & Truck Service, finally land on
Big K Radio, Red Shipley's "Rise, Shine, Feel Fine"
and pull quilts tighter around us, waiting
to hear him say, *Fauquier County schools closed,*
an eternity of Porter Wagoner's "The First Mrs. Jones,"
Conway Twitty crooning "Hello Darlin,"
and we lay in for the long haul.

I carry kindling over to the woodstove,
crumple newspaper on top of the silky bed of ashes,
throw oak twigs on top of cedar shavings,
light the paper. We hunker by the open mouth,
Laura's freckled cheeks flash orange and shadow.
Chins on knees, we listen to the hiss of paper and shavings,
George Jones and Waylon Jennings pass the minutes with us,
I add parched hickory pieces to the slow flame, watch bright
sparks like blazing dandelion heads blown
from the belly of the stove. Red calls early risers
to join the old boys at Frost's Diner for breakfast specials,
between belts of Patsy and scratchy recordings of Jimmie Rodgers,
he reads off the day's local anniversaries and Nellie Depoy's recipe
for potato salad surprise, talks about playing guitar once

with June Carter, the reduced prices at Lehew Well Drilling,
markdowns on pork butt and Domenico steaks at Glascock Grocery.

It's closing in on an hour when he lists snow totals
from Culpeper to Rixeyville, and we doze against each other,
pieces of our mother's baby dresses stitched around us,
soft quilt edges, rhythmic crack of fire and radio static,
and all around us snow covers the county,
falls against hills we'll climb and career down
later when we wake again to kettle whistle and Loretta Lynn,
familiar footfall overhead, skillets shuffled across burners,
smell of coffee and fried potatoes.
For now, we sleep at the mouth of the stove, music
of Nashville and Bristol beaming out of the farmhouse radio station
at the edge of town, above the Blue Ridge foothills, past signs
for polled Herefords and the Donut Xpress arcade and bakery.
We sleep while Red sips coffee, watches the slow stretch of dawn
through snow squalls, talks of *back in the day* as he drops
a Bill Monroe LP and plays "Footprints in the Snow,"
talks the county awake.

# Ars Poetica: Northern Virginia

I want to say it's the great blue herons
I stalk from a stealthy kayak on choppy
Occoquan waters, the barely-movement
of soda-straw legs among reservoir reeds
and rotted logs, or the way sunslant covers burgundy
yellow coreopsis sunfire flowers, deep purples
of fieldgrass and wild lilacs breeze-leaning.

But it's the asphalt and pot-holed world of Route 66,
gridlocked and loud, oily-aired 66
where a goose was struck dead, its brown-black feathers
cockeyed on one wing, turned toward traffic as if
waving. It's the slow centipede-like movement of vehicles
to the left, quieting of horns, everyone adjusting course
to let it rest there and to give wide berth to its partner
who stands almost on top of him, her white chest
pressed against his, immobile but for the head
she moves just slightly to stare at each car
as it slows and passes.

# The Preacher's Daughter Studies Her Reflection

She stands before the full-length mirror
hanging on the back of the bathroom door.
Thirteen years old and she can see
the breasts that will come heavy, the curse
of Eve that lies somewhere between legs
and neck. When she lifts her skirt,
bares herself to her reflection, she sees the place
her mother covers with a washrag
when she bathes her. The slightest lift
of one leg and she can see the edges
of vermilion sin, the folded-over place
her mother says can never be closed again
once it's unlocked. She can envision
it flinging open at the slightest provocation
of curious fingers, the prying of a wicked,
would-be woman.

She runs her fingers across the underside of breasts,
feels the way they fit against her ribs,
that smallest rib a gift from God.
Did he wrench it from Adam's side
or break it out tenderly, knowing
how bone and flesh would swell, curve
to the taunting lift of breast,
turn his prize against him?

After church, she walks the mountainsides
until she finds a crevice,
indistinct and dark, to hide the push
and pull of her body,
and slips herself deep into the musk
of some other animal's den.

# You Can't Leave It When You Go

*I cursed this place when I was young
for cursing me with a broken tongue
and hiding the horizon from my view.
These days I can't quit thinking of
the land whose shoulders blocked the sun
and people who speak music like I do.*
—Tiffany Williams

My mother's practiced tongue never gave away
the hollers, the one-room schoolhouse at the mouth
of Garden Creek, never gave away the spring house
cut in the hillside or its flat sod roof she could walk out on
from straight off the road.

When Granddaddy moved them to flat land, valley down
where his boys would find steel or wood and not
the Black Lung trap of Red Jacket and Oakwood Smokeless,
she learned ridicule quickly, tucked accent and dialect
quietly behind teeth and tongue, made herself *bookish.*
She chose paralegal over lumber secretary, put back funds,
took in her baby sister, put in a phone at her folks' house,
married an Army Yankee, taught her children
mountain harmonies, gospel sung in the car with her sister
Ruth the perfect vocal fit, two pitch pieces puzzled together
every Saturday as we drove neighborhoods,
yardsale after yardsale, piling clothes and dishes
between children, between chorus canons
of *some wondrous day,*
*when the roll is called up yonder.*

*Downhome* was said with sweet nostalgia,
with stories of Bea and Het who made her fried apple pies,
taught her to string leather breeches beans, never knotted
her toddler thread so she could *sew* at the great quilting frame.
My mother's practiced tongue never gave away
*downhome* in its totality, the little girl's belly

never quite full, payphone calls on Saturday mornings
to local jails, a child seeking answers
for her mother, a familiar drunkard's AWOL,
a *tracking down* that left her a lifelong hatred of phones,
a fear of absence.

*Downhome* was the constant background song we could hum
but never bring to full voice or lyric, things
she relegated to the margins, things
she couldn't fully push back: tears at the smell
of oranges, those rare sweet treats, or peppermint balls
that melted in our mouths and made her turn her head away,
warnings not to get in the car with Uncle Walter,
sweet as he was, or go to the woods
where our great-grandpa's still and burnt-frame house
stood long after he was gone from them.

*Downhome* was stripped of something,
of hard truths, of mountaintops long gone,
pineful stories of bootlegging and *back in the day*,
but also, sweet Jesus, also filling the stripped places
back in with younguns in that valley, piled
14-deep on stairs to sing Christmas songs
before gift-opening, to learn callouses
on tight mandolin strings, harmonies on Carter classics,
or stories of grandfathers who walked across states and mountains
to build stone walls along the Blue Ridge Parkway with the CCC,
and grandmothers who painted walnut shells and glued
pine needles and crimson leaves to wood pieces to sell
as *folk art* for shoe money, to teach herbal medicine,
dousing, mourning dove calls, and the shrill magic
of a grass blade pulled tight between thumbs,
against lips, blown into song, all the things
we wouldn't learn in classrooms they insisted on, all the things
that would follow us as they follow my mother, the salty
sweet citrus-sting of those hills and hollers,
all the meanings of the words *broken* and *blessed* and *kin*.

A man may drink and not be drunk
A man may fight and not be slain
A man may court a pretty girl
And perhaps be welcomed back again
But since it has so ought to be
By a time to rise and a time to fall
Come fill to me the parting glass
Good night and joy be with you all

# Hillbilly Transplant: Starling in Gingko

At the corner of 48th and Third Avenue, a starling
hangs dead, still clinging to a branch
halfway up a city-beaten gingko tree.
I watch it rock in the breeze, suspended
upside down like some iridescent bat
only asleep until cool evening wakes it
to right itself or drop straight to flight,
leap into the hunt for mosquitoes and junebugs.

Each day I see it still there,
only sign of time passing
the slow fall of wings,
unfolding from its body
until a week after first sighting
they are fully outstretched, underfeathers
oily and matted, a sad, feathered crucifix
hung by its base and half-gone but still
something noble in the way it holds, relentless,
day after day, the eyes sinking, pulling back
into its head, until one day I find the branch empty,
hunt in the grated square around the tree,
no sign of falcon or city cat, no bones,
only a few black feathers peppered
with shiny greens and purples lying against the dirt
and cast-off napkins, faded Chapstick tube,
and all the other discarded things.

# Hillbilly Transplant: Seeing Child on Junction Boulevard Subway Platform

The child trembled as if something bone cold
or wild with electricity had lighted on her fingers,
like someone walked across her grave, or death
was fixin to knock on her door, like Grandma said,
and like Grandma that time, mid-step in the kitchen
went stock-still, dropped that pot of soup beans,
cast iron and bean slurry marking her feet the rest of her life
and didn't move from that spot or scream, but said low as a growl,
*One of the boys is dead.*

The child trembled as if any and all of that
come to visit, but not frozen or burned or clutched
with sight, she reached fingers higher,
toward the sparks that sprayed from the N train's wheels,
sandwich wrappers from Pollo y Pollo clutching her legs
in the rush of hot Astoria air, head thrown back,
she danced one foot to the other, eyes closed, smiling
like she'd been gifted something.

# Hillbilly Transplant: Where I Live

104th and the corner pizza, rumble of subway,
the projects on Amsterdam, bodega at the corner
where Korea John sells me spicy noodles
always the same warning, "Too spicy for you, Dixie girl!"
but they're as simple as pouring hot water on them,
nights I'm home late from Hugo's too tired to cook,
belly grumbling after small plates of cilantro-peppered dishes
I choked down, too in love to tell him
it all tastes like soap in my mouth,
too tired to tell Korea John my nights
are all about the choke and burn of first city love.

# Hillbilly Transplant Writes "Where I'm From" Exercise with Imposter Narrative

City girl, Brooklyn-born, rough raised
by loud women cursing store-bought pickles,
and men who couldn't carry their own weight,
by subway tunnels where I learned to hold my breath
and perfect the hasty walk-not-run when rats
hugged the tile walls of transfers between Prospect Park
and Brighton Beach, or not-quite-men
proved themselves to each other with catalogs
of come-ons as I passed.

I am summer drought brazen-cracking the hydrants,
standing in the sting of its water until
my jeans adhered to me and the waves of heat
finally rolled off.

I am kitchen windows sweating streaks all year long,
neighborhood Babushkas who cooked constantly, sour cherry jams,
pickled garlic, my Ukrainian neighbor whose chewy black breads
I teethed on, her sister whose quick clap under my chin
taught me early to say *spasiba* to everything no matter how small I was,
no ingrates tolerated in the swarm of warm aprons, these women
who guarded the gates to every doughy, salty treat of my childhood.

I am backseat of the movies at Sheepshead Bay,
learning the indelicate truth of neighborhood boys.
I am feet whose callouses came early, concrete
and hard grass, 5th floor walk-up, my Latvian neighbor
who would only paint my nails if I let her take a razor
to my heels, the pads of my feet, and then soak them
in sudsy warm water while she talked of love.
I am my mother's Matryoshka, each doll its own lacquered red,
sun-yellows and brilliant greens, flowers of her homeland, peasant
and princess, each piece a story, a variation from that tiniest doll, a baby
fashioned from a single perfect piece of wood.

# Hillbilly Transplant: New Home

First night in Harlem,
weary from pushing Borax into corners of rooms
where hardwood falls short of walls and roaches
are sure to come, I rise from the bed at a car alarm screaming,
raise the blinds and look to the street below
where a woman squats to shit
between a black Subaru and souped-up Camry,
the spoiler pulled up on one side
where she hangs on for balance.
She throws a spent wad of tissues to the ditch beside her
and I think of childhood, my window above the bed,
my view through wild cherry leaves to the culvert
at the yard's edge, where my sister and I burned cow patties
beneath summer branches and leaves
to keep the smolder going long enough to burn
load after load of hurricane debris, where we burned
our waitress aprons one summer, the strange greasy smoke
of polyester marking our ceremony, the end of tired feet
and bad money, both of us back to college in a few days
where we would learn the things we thought would take us
far from the stink and sweat.

# Hillbilly Transplant: In 72nd Street Subway Tunnel a Meditation on Home

Drive Old Leeds Road, curve and lift
of asphalt Daddy used to speed up for, drop
our stomachs like a moment's roller coaster,
at fork of Casanova Junction, a shock
of blackberry bramble, old Nehi freezer
where used to there was a country store sold
the only black walnut ice cream in the county.

Drive past horse farms where pasture and orchard
turn open fields, the Airlie Estate where
the monied marry, where we crawled under
weak fence some nights in late spring
to night-stalk monster catfish from overstocked ponds.
Drive 605 to rutted cattle guard spots
where names meet rural routes, where horse farms
give way to small plots of corn, sustenance farms,
bricked silos and rusted tipples, down low roads
where the Thornton and Hazel Rivers meet at the foot
of Sperryville orchards, roadside stands of comb-in honey,
chow-chow and double wedding ring quilts
the tourists buy in fall. Drive the smooth, slow
wind of Skyline Drive where walls built by the CCC
still bracket the road, pull-off, and path.

Follow orange trumpet vine and wineberry bushes
till you hear the steady croon of the Shenandoah,
path of honeysuckle and black-purple pokeberry vine
to railroad ties laid into bank, creosote-soaked
staircase into cool grassy current,
let toes slide between rock shelf and riverbed,
crabcrawl where current is fast, find the place
where jutting rocks split water, the eddy and swirl
shallow enough for herons to stand watch.

Sit at the apex of water and rock,
breathe wet feather and river reed,
algae foam and mimosa blossoms.
Find stillness.

Open eyes.
Find yourself still city-gone.
Let yourself be moved
by wool coats, shouldered satchels,
unstoppable current of the mass.
Find a spot on slick metal pole.
Hold on.
Hear the whoosh as doors shut behind you.

# Hillbilly Transplant: Seed and Scatter

The prayer plant you gave me is dying.
On the windowsill overlooking 71st Street it wilts
even now with this light spring rain.
If I was a diviner, this would be the sign
that says, *Run, girl.*

First was the prayer plant—early in love,
when we were still mango and pepino dulce,
heart-shaped chirimoya and blood orange filled to bursting,
sweet sticky things that lingered on skin and tongue.
Still midday smiles at thoughts of night, Peruvian flutes
and flamenco guitar in the background, our bodies
moving dark over light.

First was the prayer plant—before the table
you grabbed at a parking lot auction in Alphabet City,
or the handmade candle, cornflower blue
and lavender, big as the Inca Cola bottle mold,
before the pin from Lima I suspect was really
for someone else, the one you put in a leather pouch
you made from old boots, laced with sinew,
my initials burned onto that tight brown skin
with a heated paperclip.

First was the prayer plant—a cutting
from the wooden planter perched
on your radiator, a birthday gift
you set down inside a terra cotta pot,
worked the soil as you rehomed it,
covered the excised roots over,
pushed until nothing moved, explained
in both languages as you pressed my body,
soil still on your hands, how those soft oval leaves
turn upward, *abierto*, at night, back down again

with sun break, sultry murmur
against neck and collarbone.

First was the prayer plant—before nights
of too much rum and pisco, late arrivals,
your late-night reconnaissance
trolling online for a younger body while mine,
all 30 years of it, still hummed in your bed,
love-drunk and willfully blind to ever-refilling glasses
of vodka-heavy chicha morada, to anything
beyond the sight of you cooking rice in clay pots
you brought back from your hometown in Cusco,
the classical guitar against your bare chest reclined on the sofa,
oil canvasses you painted that covered the bedroom walls—
gitanos and toreros, my favorite behind the bed, a flamenco dancer,
crimson and cobalt skirts painted mid-arc, arms
above her head, eyes closed, her perfect gypsy body
poised in sweaty ascension.

First was the prayer plant—and last,
last was the rain-soaked midnight walk
from 98th and Broadway to the subway, that final
humiliation of being put out
not with a fury or a passion
but with an assault of indifference, a disinterest
no artist's canvas could unmar.

I should bring the plant back inside.
It did nothing to me, after all.
But there is something cleansing in the dropping,
one by one, of these leaves, their pale green and fuchsia
slapped against the marble sill by this surging rain.

# Hillbilly Transplant: Pondering Park Dominoes and the Death of Celia Cruz

*July 16, 2003*

In other places, slick, smooth plastic clatter
across family formica tables,
bright white bars and black divots
so round and perfect they might hold
plump orange caviar, a smattering
of pepper and sea salt,
or seat for pungent capers.
But across the boroughs,
in Far Rockaway, Bensonhurst, Washington Heights,
Saturday streets smell of sweet onions,
barbacoa, huancaina, the parks
with their chess tables convert to dominoes,
old Dominican men and Eastern European boys
sit to a game, pieces move in careful
patterns, groups of men on either side
sweat and chatter and gesture.
No language barrier, they speak in forehead slaps
of flawed moves, claps on the back when it's well done.
Plates of grilled vegetables, brick oven breads
and meats spiced from oceans apart passed
around both sides of the table bring fingers to lips,
groans of appreciation.

There is no shared language for grief,
but there is food, so plates of ropa vieja,
rice and sofrito are laid across the tables,
dominoes put away, heads nod, hips salsa
as Celia Cruz's smoky voice carries from speakers
across the parks, from parked cars lining Lenox Avenue,
air split with timbale and great belling brass notes,
and even the youngest of European boys grins
and finds the words to "La Negra Tiene Tumbao,"

the old Ukrainian men shout *Azucár!*
and grasp the forearms of the Cubans,
cheering them when the dominoes
are brought back out, smacking their lips
in approval as they move pieces, clack
and clatter lifting again beneath guitar and claves.

# Hillbilly Transplant: Working at the Metropolitan Opera

First month, I run my hands against those burgundy,
crushed velvet walls lined with portraits of Caruso and Callas,
swoon when Placido Domingo holds the elevator for me,
and again when I hear the early rehearsal for *La Boheme*
through the old RCA speaker perched on a shelf in my office.

Second month, I invent errands to run,
lose myself to the maze of hallways beneath the stage.
Something akin to Alice in Wonderland, each hall
is shorter than the next, the ceiling lower and lower
until the giant coffin-sized case of a symphony bass
has to stand at a pitch, propped sideways against a piano
just to fit. Each hall lined with racks of costumes
seems stranger than the next, Verdi-inspired props, a huge
bird costume from *The Marriage of Figaro,* ballerinas
from the Bolshoi scatter at my footfall, exit a side room
toward me, a billow of contraband smoke rushing
out from behind them. They wear heated slippers,
legwarmers that accentuate their heart-shaped calves.

Third month, I ponder the $7 cafeteria clamshell
of mostly arugula and tiny scoop of tuna, wonder
how close I am to maxing out that last card, how much
we could save in rent if we called the walled-off part
of our living room a bedroom, sell some other artist
the dream of living on Broadway, neglect to mention
the subway directly under us or the projects on Amsterdam
on the other side of the block. Finish tuna while listening
to stagehands and set designers talk union politics.
Make grocery list, wonder how far $40 will stretch, wonder
how many bags I can carry the six blocks from Gristedes
back to the apartment. Wonder if it will rain on me.

Fourth month, tally two-year debt, take lunch
in my office, skip cafeteria, skip courtyard performance
of Juilliard musicians, turn dial of my RCA speaker to *off*
when the soft tremolo mandolin of *Don Giovanni*
leaves me hand-over-mouth crying,
a barrage of homesick images: family reunions,
great-uncles plucking mandolins cradled on their broad chests,
picking guitars, banjos, everyone foundering
in lawn chairs in that pressing Virginia heat,
pregnant, always, with rain and threat of storm.
No amount of staring out the floor to ceiling windows
at the grand fountain or City Ballet in Lincoln Square
can disenthrone those faces or voices, singing
mountain ballads, hymns, and Stanley Brothers standards,
sweaty hands clasped, voices perfectly imperfect,
soul-savingly beautiful, my heart's familiar redemption.
I know as sure as I've known anything here,
that I will leave this city and its grandeur, return South,
settle in a tree-laden space with mountains around me
and no doubt dream of crushed velvet walls
and halls filled with bel canto runs and ballerinas.

# Contrapuntal: Driving as the Flood Comes

Over the Susquehanna rain rushes
from low-lying clouds
an egret perches a sycamore branch
and a black snake coils the road lane line
everything rushing past it
one eye on purple phlox and Japanese anemone,
an ear this day for full-bellied music
the Salve Reginas, Prokofiev double-bass and belled brass
at the highwater surge
sandbags beside
chances, all the stacked things
now is the time—
take a leap

An osprey
along country roads
over turbulent water below
as if to strike
and so we keep one eye on it,
roll down car windows, turn up the volume
for the dramatic pieces
booming until windows rattle and
all along the river's edge
johnboats, as if someone was unsure the
outcome balanced in whether
to fight or float
in the churning current

Of all the comrades that e'er I had
They're sorry for my going away
And all the sweethearts that e'er I had
They'd wish me one more day to stay

# Benefaction

## I.

He reaches long arms into the current, steadies himself
against high points of rock, searches out footing on slick
algae-covered riverbed, shifting shelf I warned him about
when I suggested an innertube to hold for balance.
His hulking figure finally gets deep enough to settle
center of gravity and I watch the flick and retrieve
of carefully tied fly-bait as he twists and rocks,
his mouth pursed with effort to flush out
the bass or crappie he plans to feed us tonight.
I sit chest-deep, closer to the shore in an old lawnchair,
pale orange, lime green, and white webbing that has scratched
the backs of my legs all my life, but its old aluminum legs
hold up still against the Shenandoah pushing at my back.
I wave as he moves farther out, heads around a bend
where I told him my father used to catch citation bass,
rivercats big as his arm.

## II.

As children Laura and I perched ourselves
in these lawnchairs, under shade of inlets
hulked by silver maples and Carolina willows, water
only to knees' depth while our father
stalked smallmouth bass and waved at his girls,
both of us perfectly happy to sit
with bags of corn chips and cheese waffles
in cool-water coves, minnows pecking at legs and feet,
too quick for orange-dusted fingers
though we never gave up trying.

Long drives from home to river
in Dad's beater truck were shortened
by the sweaty excitement of salty goodies
and sweet Yoo-Hoos in the cooler.
This was the place where sweltering August
met cool, silky water, where we watched blue herons
and kingfisher hunt the shorelines, where we knew
we were *grown up* when finally trusted to lift
the minnow netting from the low-water bridge,
to pull up Dad's bait, silver and flopping.
This was the place we shared secrets when we were older
and thought we knew it all, floated on innertubes and rafts talking plans,
talking dreams, eating throwback treats and drinking
those strange almost-chocolate Yoo-Hoos, not a single care beyond
clearing jutting rocks with our rafts and watching for cottonmouths.

III.

A rainshower moves across the river in one gust,
blows the range of Blue Ridge toward Luray
and he reappears, raising the stringer from the water,
several fish dangling. I can see his smile from here.
He wades over to me, leans on aluminum arms,
kisses me hard, the river's salty gifts still gifting.

This is not a place I share outside my kin.
This is not a place I take a lover, no matter how far gone.
This is a gift from a guarded heart, though I know this man
in the bend of river with me doesn't fully understand that.
Not yet.

# Under the Sugar Moon

Path of gnarled, knotting birch root
pushed up in pervasive, tangled tree webs,
scarcely a place for footfalls, but we walk it
at day's dimming, chase the gloaming,
when the heat haze has burned off
and we climb our way to pond perimeter
to perch a humped juneberry root, watch
for osprey to deadweight themselves from branches,
dive till they are just above surface and pitch up,
talons plunging the water to pull
unsuspecting bluegill from beneath.
We watch this till mosquitos have peppered us,
sound of flesh smacking flesh,
slapping the stealthy ones from each other's legs,
no one but us and what luminesces
from the hulking Sugar Moon, what calls
the sap and maple to life, to swell and spill
sticky sweet over early spring lovers
tangled in root and fern, phosphorescent foxfire,
all things breathless and incandescent.

# Under the Flower Moon: What We Plant

*May 2011*

We lie in a soft green patch, moss oasis
surrounded by tall russet fieldgrass
we can just see through to the sycamores reaching
long finger-bone branches to glassy Shenandoah surface,
parting the crystalline rush, a perfect V on either side.
I trace the V at the base of your neck, cleft in your chin.
We sleep under a waxing new moon, bright, brief crescent above us
and you whisper, *The new moon rises when the sun rises,*
*crosses the sky with the sun, sets when the sun sets,*
*a perfect pairing so overshadowed by light*
*that we can't see it until it moves away.*

I know nothing of lunar longitudes but tell you my people planted
by the signs, by the moons, this next full is the Flower Moon,
fifth moon of Creation when plants show their spirit sides
for all the world to see. You hold yourself above me, still
as I speak my grandma's words, *You plant things that flower above ground*
*on the waxing new moon, the young moon, the crescents*
*calling the beans up the poles and tomatoes to the vines.*
When you move again, we are water and earth,
moss and river, we plant between us, that crescent growing fatter
each day, moving back toward the point of fullness
before it slips and is lost again
to the glare and blaze of its pairing.

# Tracer

There is no subtle tracing of your body when you sleep,
no amount of exhaustion or satiation that puts you down
deeply enough for someone's hands to touch you unnoticed,
and so I have wondered at your closed eyes when I trace that scar
on your left side just beneath that last small rib, its edges jagged
and raised where your brothers field-stitched you in haste
after a *policeman* there to guide you to the local jirga
stabbed you in your sleep while his colleagues jumped the others.
Smitty told me you broke the man's neck
before you were even fully awake,
that the three of you took down the whole of them, stacked them
like cordwood, egressed to a safety point
where field medics gave you morphine,
tried to clean up the mess made of you.
You have told me none of this.
When I kiss the raised smooth edge of it, you lift my head and pull me
up and over you, brush the huge pads of your thumbs against my eyelids
as if to erase what might linger beneath.

# Heaving

At the edge of Ft Bragg, pre-dawn, the haloed shapes of Christmas lights
are bent in the fog of this unseasonably warm weather.
You don't offer promises of unscathed returns
or apologies for the tears I soak your shirtfront with
but step back, finally, hold the back of my neck with one hand,
the other pressed flat against my chest
and then you're gone.
The fog twists the wake behind you,
your long stride leaves cyclonic traces that lift and sink
against the pavement long after I've lost you
in the whole-swallow of mist blinking misshapen red and green stars.

The path back to the car is flanked by evergreens
burdened with spray-snow from locals who finally
gave up on a real winter, and I stop to look down on the pale green tips
of daffodils sprouting defiantly against railroad ties, the strange smell
of creosote and loam carried up in misty droplets
that hang on me to the parking lot.
Condensation on the windshield casts snaking shadows
against the passenger seat I lean toward, your scent still resting there.
If I came back here in a week, two, would the yellow ruffle
of daffodils play strange backdrop to the last of the Christmas props,
or would they lie bent-bladed and cut down with weather
that must surely come?

I leave the post remembering how I walked the blustery edge
of fields with Grandma who snapped frozen heads of tulips, filling
her coat front, folded toward her belly, swollen
with the waxy, glistening yellows and pinks, still bullet-headed
before they could open, taken out by a killing frost.
*We call this heaving,* she said, placing one of the icy
smooth things in my palm. *Get a winter cycle doesn't come fierce enough
to freeze the ground through, every hopeful seed will try to flower.*

# Deployment: Homefront

On my knees beside the sunken tub,
I've sprayed a straight line of cleaner
across the porcelain base and halfway
across the tub on that first swipe, brush bearing down,
I see the faint outline
of your foot, yank the brush back and push
the bleach bare-handed from that piece of you,
phantom and unexpected.
I press my hand flat, palm to your heel,
my fingers fitting easily
to the instep not quite
to the pads of your toes,
leave it there until the slow burn
of bleach begins and I pull back,
one thin line where my forefinger rested
etched to your sole.

# At the VA

He meets the guard opening first doors.
He knows JoBeth the receptionist will be there
in 5, 4, 3, 2.
He takes the coffee filters she hands him.
He nods good morning as staff file in.
He puts eight scoops of coffee in the filter basket.
He pauses before hitting the ON button.
He knows it will turn on with a *click*
not a *bang.*
He hesitates anyway.
He steadies his hand and pushes it on.
He sits in the chair closest to the door.
He sits with his back to the wall.
He sits where he can see
everyone in the world.

# Beautiful

You propose in a hotel lobby just off Ft Bragg,
hold up a pink poster with an ARMY WIFE bumper sticker
and the word YES in all caps, three question marks after it.

We have fifteen hours before you are due back on base, off
again downrange, your last *hardship tour.*
I wake against you ten minutes before the alarm goes off,

go through the familiar memorization, my head pounding
with adrenaline and the need to commit it all, to close my eyes
months later and remember how to conjure you completely.

It's a quick, easy inventory over planes of your stomach, worked tight
and unyielding with heavy packs on your back, the higher curve
of your thighs when you've been in mountainous areas, the cleft

in your chin where I once nicked you when you let me
shave your weekend beard, both of us
wiping pink-tinged Barbasol from us.

What takes longer is the catalog I can't stop myself making.
Left side, just beneath the shortest rib where the skin rises a sleek,
jagged line where they field-stitched a stabwound: Paktika.

The grafted place on the inside of your left arm where no hair will grow,
where an RPG stung you as it passed by, a near miss: Ramadi.
Right upper thigh, two-inch scar hard landing in a Chinook: Fallujah.

Left lower calf, three-inch scar: Pristina, Kosovo.
Right clavicle, small scar that makes the pattern of hair appear wavy
tamped down, a strange crop circle I asked about once
and you said simply *Africa.*

You are watching me when I look up.
I lie flush against you, kiss the smooth spot beneath your right ear
where a parachute line burned you once as you spun
somewhere above the Earth.

You say, *Talk me awake, wife. I want to take your voice with me.*
I press my fingers against the rough scar at your collarbone, feel your pulse
push back against me. *In Japan,* I whisper, *when they mend broken things*
*they aggrandize the damage by filling the cracks with gold.*
*They believe when something has suffered damage and has a history,*
*it becomes more beautiful.*

# Cleave

The world makes no distinction
between the knife that parts the wall
or sorts the army your heart has built,
or the one that makes room and way
for love, that open space we fill with nights
by the creek or sprawled on quilts
to watch the Perseids fall above us.

The world makes no distinction
between *that* knife and the one
that will pierce to spill and fall, dash
against rock and river, draw open miles
of vascular roads that wind from heart
to wrist or what you want to spill
to the earth like dust from that box,
from that pewter box
to slick river-grassed water, the knife
that parts the water around rock and stump
and red oak rise, around heron's legs
and a hundred years of leaf rot
or the rock that covers our wedding bands
where I tied them together and pushed them
in a birch leaf beneath the sulfur-marked stone
beneath a split-trunk cottonwood whose lean
shelters all the shaded things we sat beneath and in.

But since it fell unto my lot
That I should rise and you should not
I gently rise and softly call
Good night and joy be to you all

# Zebras Through the Fire

*for Myron*

*When fires sweep the savannahs in Africa, most animals perish trying to run
from the fire until they drop from exhaustion and are overtaken. Many zebras
survive because they run toward the fire and ultimately through or around it.*

I.

From above, the char across burned savannah
looks a black river, come lower and it looks
an artist's smudge, deliberate and pulled
to the canvas edge.

From space, it is a black scar on a golden face,
the kind that stubbles badly, like that place
on your left jawline where some stint in country left you
marked, a pause in beardline, a dash, a hyphen
as if something was to follow.

II.

From space, you don't see the scorched hump
of thorn acacia trees that hiss and pop,
each one drawing in on itself, bent toward the fiery ground,
a gnarled hand closing itself to rhinos and impalas
used to feeding on the sweet spiraled pods,
cowering now, eyes wild as wind,
flames taking them where they fall,
the miles they ran behind them swallowed
in great gulping flashes, everything left raw and unsheltered,
soot and skeleton.

III.

Yours was a closed service, discrete and honorable,
two dozen of us crammed beneath a single valley oak

withered in 100-degree heat and the surreality of that meager box
with its pewter top, your name punched into it.

I can think of nothing but burning savannahs,
ground covered with char ash and bone dust,
pieces of wood still orange-tipped as they twist the air like burning paper,
like the windhorses of Tibet, like paper prayers cast to the mountains.
Zebras, shaken and frothy-mouthed from running, from seared lungs,
but standing at the burnt edges where trees are still green-leafed.

Your brother chokes into his fist behind me.

From space we are nowhere beneath that tree,
not even a spot in that green-brown smudge
at the edges of our country, no distinctions
between those standing and those fallen.

# Painting of Grief: Exhibit of Aztec Goddess at the Met

Tlazolteotl, filth-eater, goddess of marred repute,
all that we would excise you from if only
your face was familiar enough to pick you
from the crowd, distinguish your godliness
from the bent bodies of women on Amsterdam Avenue
who comb the trashcans and swallow down
the cast-off, the wasted, the unwanted.
Would your face hold a thousand furrows
where dirt and shit have settled, a grimace
of permanent revulsion at what you place
inside a mouth so square, so hinged and ready
for the next awful bite that it has given over
to the inevitable and left itself gaping—or
would you have the leathered face of sun,
of toil and land, coal tattoos and farmer's markings,
sorrowful eyes that say you've seen enough
but know there is always more yet to come?

Goddess of purification, of redemption, eater of grief,
bringer of things to expunge and expel what ails us.
You are those vile treebark teas that draw the sick from us,
poultices of pungent, wild root and animal tallow.
You are here in those things we take to the body
chasing relief, in our need to sate, to cool the fever
or quell the heartache, that balm of things
taken to mouth when there is nothing left
but to consume our own grief, bend
supplicant to it, mouths seeking to claim
what is already us or a return to us,
dust to dust, those mourners at southern funerals,
dirt-eaters who scoop the earth and shaled rockwalls
past lips that, bowed with sorrow, will form
a perfect O of reprieve, if only long enough
to take in what might be thrown over the dead
or trampled underfoot.

# Hillbilly Transplant: Bethesda Fountain, Central Park

Three hours after the towers fell,
alone at the Angel of the Waters Fountain,
no mimes play the sidewalk's edge like tightrope, no
queens from Chelsea rollerskate choreographed numbers, no
people at all, no sound but the elm leaves
twisting against each other,
metallic smoke in their tops, and the strange, rhythmic tapping
of a grackle who whips a piece of popcorn in its beak
against the fountain's edge, breaks off kerneled pieces
to gulp down, bits of white cast-off landing on the water, sinking
finally to rest on pennies and nickels,
a thousand slick wishes lying still.

I return months later, look up through the angel's wings, acid-rain-worn
and white with pigeon shit. It appears without sound, an airliner,
its wings like a goose pointed counter to the angel's.
I watch as it disappears behind one granite wing, hold my breath
the few seconds it takes to emerge past the angel's wingtip, feathered out
like saw teeth, still soaring, still airborne, moving sure
as I feel the ground beneath me, sure as this shifting wind that blows
dust and ash that settle against the back of the angel's downcast head,
and against my own.

# In Ithaca Reflecting on the Death of Poet Kathryn Stripling Byer

I walk the trail to Taughannock Falls, wander
down onto rock bed where divets and pocks
hold pooled water, oak pollen beads, reflection
of sky and rock canyon wall, think of you
in flowing skirt, glasses perching your head,
humming Emmylou or Dolly, some bright scarf
of teals and aquamarine, stones and corals dangling
from ears or resting against soft clavicle, a lace shawl,
crimson or purple pashmina draped over shoulders I leaned into
for comfort and love and so I dip my fingers
in the warm water, trace against dry rock
two belled hoops like earrings, a wet heart
around your initials—KSB—and watch
each loop and line disappear slowly in the sun's kiss.

# Hillbilly Transplant Finds No Frame of Reference

*Manhattan, October 7, 2001*

Jane talks about drills
they taught her as a child in the 60s:
duck and cover under school desks, fear
palpable as chalk dust on sunrays
scattered across the floors where she crouched
beneath the safe metal legs.

I have no lesson to prepare me
for the awful shaking of buildings,
all of us crouched on sidewalks
as F15s broke the air around us,
low enough to see numbers on wingtails,
or leaps made in desperation from those
heights, so unthinkable I said out loud,
*They're pieces of the building.*
There is no way to unsee this.

I dream everything is falling: birds
from perches blasted with debris, faces
of buildings slipping like Dali paintings at the Met,
the sun's annular edges pulling down and out
as if splattered against the clear blue
or dashed against the sidewalk.

# Thus Always to Tyrants

I.

Third grade, Miss Betty Rhodes' class,
we try our first taste of dead language,
bold, white-lettered Latin,
a crescent beneath the state seal,
our flag, our motto:
*Sic Semper Tyrannis.*

Recite, repeat, a chorus of small Virginia kids,
we roll the sibilant phrase, on the playground
we make stabbing motions with sticks, shout
*Tyrants! Tyrants!*

II.

Once at a family reunion, Uncle Ralph, one eye glassy and tilted, lost
in World War II, tried to explain how far men will go
to save what they think needs saving,
to kill who they think needs killing.
He pulled a wad of tobacco from his cheek and threw it
to the ground between us, looked me square and said,
*Men like to make heroes and big stories out of bloodletting.*
*Like to build theirselves marble statues.*
*Man's smartest when he finds a bit of land and grows things out of it,*
*gets hisself as far downrange from that foolishness as he can.*

III.

Under a blistering California sun,
they hand me a box of ashes.
There is no battlefield for this, no markers,
not even a headstone. Just this box, its shiny lid
polished over those ten letters I run my fingers against

for months, the Braille of grief I linger in until I can muster
what I know to be true, what Uncle Ralph knew to be true:
better to cast him to a sycamore wind, to the Shenandoah's current,
to the things that will lift and flow and carry this piece of him
to a bit of land where something might take root, grow him
into something beautiful.

# Hillbilly Transplant: Upper West Side, October 10, 2001

A woman carries a fresh baguette
from the Hot 'N Crusty on 71st and Broadway,
flinches slightly at the sound of a jet going over.
She does not look up.

It is cold today, the feeling
of true fall in the air, the wind shifts,
blowing the smell of burned things
away from us, web-thin shroud floating
out over the Hudson, the only sign
the panicked flight of seagulls rushing
to stay ahead of it.

# Smoke, Salt, Sweet

*Manhattan, September 28, 2001*

Burnt metal still stings the nostrils
weeks later, drifts on perverse winds,
settling into flag stripes, sometimes random pieces
of paper, still charred or rain-wrinkled and stuck
to building sides, all the still-upright things
that gather and hold.

But for all the shattered and shuttered things,
wooden crates at the Fairway Market
still line the storefront and I touch dusky apricots,
sunny lemons and purple eggplants,
red and yellow peppers, bin after box after crate
of cucumbers, kale, and radish,
brown and red onions still sloughing skin onto Yukons
and Idahos beneath them.

I walk to O'Donnell's pub and Robin
has a corner table at the window
where we can watch the sidewalks
and sky over mugs of black
and tan that sweat the wood grain,
small plates of aged gouda, pocked and nutty,
an applewood-smoked gruyere and deeply orange
Vermont cheddar, a fuchsia stripe of Portofino red,
crooked and imperfect.

We watch the silenced TV in the corner, its banner
still scrolling estimates of casualties, something
about a dirty bomb radius, but I am intent
on the soppressata and wild boar salami delivered to us,
brick red and fatty speckled,
pungent as any wild thing left to its own devices,
and Robin says, *I'll bet this is what it tastes like*

*to wander the woods rooting for acorns and hickories.*
I don't tell her those boars
would trample her and eat everything
but her belt buckle.

The next plate, a perfectly symmetrical circle
of prosciutto-wrapped melon, ebony pools
at the edges, a balsamic reduction
to dredge the sweet, salty bites through.
Peter Jennings' face appears in the background,
then a random person showing how to seal a window
with duct tape in case of another anthrax attack.
We watch his mouth move, a familiar muted thing, until
we've had enough and walk the few blocks where
the bread and sugared air is a path, a reprieve,
the tiny Italian café where there are no TVs, just
the orderly crowd, everyone leaning into glass cases,
Neopolitans and glazed fruit tortas rearranged and replaced,
pistachio biscottis, pignolatas, lemon and orange crocettes,
the frozen cases of bright pink gelatos and chicory brown spumoni.
We settle on a chocolate amaretto cake, admire the dusting
of confectioner's sugar and raspberry glaze,
slow ourselves in our final bites,
linger over the plate, push tines into last crumbs,
watch the sidewalks and sky, the locals
who hold each other's elbows
as they speak.

# Observations of Escape

*for Aunt Linda*

An osprey drafts thermals
that gust across Blue Ridge peaks, up from
the pulse of Rappahannock river and rock,
bug backs and fish scale scintillate with sun strokes
and water breaks catch his eye, turn wings
to bank left, dive earthward, talons splayed.
Sunfish scatter, race for rock-shelf cover
where floor bottom is dappled,
the petal of a wild cherry blossom floats the current,
casts a shadow the fish track
as they wait in rock shade, tails
in perpetual fan motion, water over gills,
shadow-watching, all the things
that land and pass
or circle and circle.

# Memorial Day

I turn on the radio, hear news
of predicted meteor showers tonight.
I wonder at the falling of constellations,
those things that guide and give us our bearings.

I watch the pitch sky, follow
the arc of meteors as they blaze
for just a moment and are gone.
I smile, imagine him saying,
*Our bodies are made up of collapsed stars.*

I trace a vein across the top of my hand,
find strange comfort to wonder
what internal navigation comes
of a body made from broken pieces,
every cell, every pulsing, quaking thing
the cast-off and remnants of the dying
or the dead.

# [Us]

Consider us mathematical,
our story an open interval
that can't contain its endpoints,
must not contain
its beginning
or its end.

Bind this story.
Seal it in silent bookends
because if you gave me
our beginning, it would be all
inaugural fumbling of hands,
circling each other in arguments,
alarm clocks set hours apart, scowl
of sleep interrupted.
That bookend holds the first
night terrors in a shared bed,
the only time I ever feared him
or saw him tremble.
You can keep that shit.

If you gave me our end?
I would have to dredge up
the static of that phone call, the one
that dropped twice before it connected,
or my sisters' faces when they reached me
across the country in Denver,
or the instructions
on what could be said,
on what could not.

If you gave me our end?
There would be no answers in that small
pewter box, nobody

to show me the difference between
spouse and betrothed.

If you gave me our end, unbounded?
It would still say,
*I cannot write this thing.*

But the infinite between outset and culmination?
Hell yes.
Every green ash he ran his fingers across
on the banks of the Rappahannock, every steak
he undercooked just the way I love it, every
off-key Irish ballad he attempted to impress me with
before he knew I was a musician.
The first and only poem I wrote him.
His useless trivia I am still filled with,
*Did you know Germans call grasshoppers hay horses?*
Every smirk when I said, *Yes, I knew that.*
The stalk of Virginia bluebells he plucked once
and brushed against my arm.
Late night recitations of trees we'd seen.
His thesaurus, dog-eared and cracked-spine
where I find that a synonym for *ending* is *catastrophe,*
but it is also *summation, completion.*

So steal the alpha and omega of us.
The everything-between came in those
rounded months we watched Perseids fall
from our quilt in spring fields or wandered
Bull Run claiming all the trees as I claim them now
because our story is chestnut and redbud,
buttonwood and saskatoon, rock-slip
through Spout Run, and the night-sky app
we put on both phones, set to his locations
so I could cipher what his eyes rested on
those nights on the other side of the world.
Our story is the app on my phone still,
still set to a thousand other skies.

# Solace: What Slips the Horizon

*for Jackson & Peyton*

This canal, maroon-brown as a strong tea,
Waccamaw River and Socastee Creek water
so slow to move that I take picture after picture
of hulking conifer reflections, their bulbed branches
suddenly shimmied and gone as turtle heads break
the surface with their slow blink, shellbacks glisten
orange and black in this last sun.

Geese honk from the bank beneath my balcony,
call to others as they swim up the canal,
send mallards and their ducklings scattering
beneath bank laurel and river shrubs.

Breeze of magnolia blossom and spider lilies shake
Spanish moss that hangs the low oak branches,
bats dot purpling sky above the water,
dive and snatch bugs from the air, pluck
the last skimmers whose long-legged dance
almost made the shore.

Crescendo of frogs who hiccup their songs,
call to love or just to sing in praise of sunset,
slow slide of heat from porch and yard, across shrub
and river to fields of burnt grass that light golden
for just a moment as sunlight licks across them, splits
spokes of fiery orange and deep siennas through oaks
and palms before it disappears, pulls the heat
back into cauldron or hole or belly
of whatever lies beneath field and horizon.

# Pandemic Months

I sit on the screened-in porch
listen to windchimes covered in KN95 masks
soaking the UV light for days to kill whatever might
still cling to them. Every breeze twists the white
cones, hanging by earstraps, the brass chimes
clanging clumsy perfect chords.
A goshawk sits on a high branch of the winged elm
Laura and I shook ice from just a few weeks ago, some
of the unsavable limbs still strewn across dried leaves.
I've lined the hickories and oaks with suet baskets
stuffed with granola and berries, peanut butter
and sunflowers. The waxwings and sparrows are agile
and quick, popping up into air
with any rustle or large breeze, settling
again to seeds in the grass, but the mourning doves
are cumbersome to land or take off, a flurry
of cooing sounds and wings flapping
like they've never been used.
The hawk descends and returns to its limb with empty talons.
Azalea bushes lining the porch bounce and rattle
with juncos and wrens who titter softly and share branches,
too smart to take eyes off that shadow
that moves between limb and lawn.

# Pandemic Months: And Still All Around Us

*for Chris Holt*

Five Forks Road curves a thread
through a needle of gold coreopsis,
fields of wild mustard and still-green wheat.
A Black man in a porch rocker,
children beside the train tracks pulling up
black-eyed Susans and purple spiderwort.

Past Briery Creek a hickory stump
covered in bright orange trumpet vine
and low-hanging branches of pink-blossomed
rose of Sharon, a white cross someone fashioned
from fence post, a hand-painted name
in perfect purple cursive.

Deep rust zinnias bend under dusty
monarchs and blue-black swallowtails,
everyone sipping what they can in this drought,
ruby-throats at sugar water feeders, dew-covered clover.

When rain comes, it rushes the valley,
a sluice through loose dirt that carries away
blood-red leaves off the sweetspire, indigo crush
of larkspur and cornflower, spiky white honeybells,
folds of myrtle and morning glories, brown leaves
off tired hickories, a torrent of all the fallen things.

I drive county roads by swollen ponds thick
with yellow-orange jewelweed sparkling still
with rainwater, watch a bass break the surface
to gulp down fallen cicada.
Cornstalks unfurl their leaves, reach skyward.
Steam gropes its way up blade and stem, lays heavy at grass top,
bends even the sturdiest stalk, one blade against another,

the collective lean seems to tilt the ground in one direction.
Willows slowly lift saturated limbs from the ground,
everything foundered and drying in the breeze that comes
like something scrubbed clean—almost.

# Flash

*May 25, 2020*

Scientists say
the parts of the brain which store memory
are the last affected by oxygen loss
and so we get near-instantaneous playback,
when that car veers off the road
or we plunge suddenly from on high
knowing, by God, it's over.
It's through.

What would flash in scenes once
my body knew, as it does, when
death is descending?
Every quilt-wrapped night
on someone's lap as a child,
full-belly meals and garden harvest,
a thousand permitted touches, a lifetime
of *I love you,* of applause
and safety and casual adventures?
How much would 9 minutes and 30 seconds
afford me? 570 seconds, 570 flash-
bangs of family, of *Mama,*
*Mama,*
*I'm through.*

I don't fucking know.
But it would all be soft
if it were mine.

If it were mine, that last microsecond: that cop
would be on the other side of the street,
other side of the town,
and my neck
unmarred,
my breath
always unobstructed.
Even this page
I can walk away from.

# Republic 2017-2020

*The sound we do not hear lifts the gulls off the water.*
—Ilya Kaminsky, *Deaf Republic*

What ear hears the dog bark a warning from yard
or woods, but not the executioner's gun?

The deaf—who we call *impaired*—know
not to turn away, know
self-preservation and mercy aren't the kissing cousins
the church would say they are, the Christ-vanished clucking
of eye-averters to children in cages, stuffing the benches full
of the like-minded, gladhanding the near-hysteria
of political pulpits, covet robes and verdicts in exchange
for children in tin foil blankets, toddlers
snatched past the margin of record, disappeared,
or washed up
face down
on the banks and shores.
The deaf know copper-laced air to be red
without looking.
Do not turn away.
Note the executioner when he comes
in his tie and lapel-pin patriotism.
Note which direction the gun is pointed, my friends.
As the story goes, if the townspeople had run at him
at once, all together, no shot would've been fired,
nothing spilled to pavement or detention floors, the gulls
would still sleep on pier poles
in air unbroken.

# Cannery in Seasons

*for my cousins*

*Summer*

Hide and seek, a perfect asylum,
place to cool a sweaty body
on damp concrete floor, tuck back
between musty, bent-boarded
shelves of white half-runner beans, peach
halves, chow-chow jars that slosh cardinal
red and lush green, pluck a small jar
of bread and butters to press chilled glass
against cheek and forehead, watch the door
through liquid shift of celery seed, clove,
and crisp cucumber, everything sealed,
sheltered.

*Fall*

Run fingers over squat jars
their bellies a raised glass lattice
that glows amber in sunshaft,
sulfured sorghum that shifts
a lazy wave when tilted, jars
of pear and apple butter,
burnt siennas and cinnamon speckled,
golden orange butternut squash, pumpkin
and carrot toward shelf-back, straw baskets
filled with sturdy gourds and Indian corn.
Move straight-back chair from yard, sit
between cedar barrels to string shucky beans,
door open to watch leaf-fall, listen
for winter in the branch-clatter of pin oak
and winged elms.

*Winter*

Heavy enough for their own shelf,
generous jars of venison, pork, and tenderloin rest
in their own fat, what they would call
*confit* in a good restaurant.
Pull jars of pale pearl onions and pickled beets,
choose from row after row of pinto beans,
sweet relish, sacks of meal and flour
from covered barrels—
*hunkering* food.
These are the meals of fireplace-sitting,
of clock-tick evenings when cold presses to bone
and stillness calls for thick breads and bowls
of steaming soup and stews heavy with game.
Touch these shelves with reverent hands.
These shelves house jars of *you will make it,*
*there is enough,* and *next year we will put back more.*


*Spring*

Cherrywood-smoked catfish and jars
of rainbow trout for March, a signal
to winter that we're pulling out of her
sleepy reach, toward all the ice breaks
and snow melt, the drying out and fresh bud,
last killing frost, and all the signs we will plant by.
Collect rocket and dewberries before deer and birds.
First jars filled are greens and cabbage, eggs peeled
and placed in beet-purple brine.
Open window.
Pull chair from between cedar barrels,
sit in doorway.
Pay attention.
Fire-throated warblers call down from hemlocks,
a skink warms itself on mountain rock, tiny squirrels
chase each other, a cacophony of dried leaves underfoot.

Pollinators move on daffodils and tulips at the cannery's edge
and a long-beaked flicker snatches grubs beneath him.
Mind all the birdcall and budding that map your path
and plan for soil beneath you, all the things you will grow
and pluck, boil down and can to fill jars on the shelves behind you,
empty now but for pink-blossom reflections
of arbutus and chartreuse hickories.

So fill to me the parting glass
And drink a health whate'er befall
And gently rise and softly call
Good night and joy be to you all

# Passing of Grief

*for Scott*

Your boots in the corner of the closet
slump against hardwood where you left them by the door,
where *I* left them by the door, that cracking sound
they made when lifted from that hard, still place,
something giving way.

Canoe through Shenandoah current where
river is just river and sun on my shoulders
a reminder of all that bears down to grow
the green of sycamores and saskatoon to shade
and tame heat that bounces back off water
I rest my fingers against, silken tangle
through skeins of river grass you may
have settled against when we scattered you here,
all the inlet shrubs, white ash and sugar maples,
all the herons' nests you might have wound yourself into,
or tiny moving things you might be bone or scale
or wing of now.

Canoe tied to the truck roof myself,
knots of rope I have learned these last years,
air filter I can pull from my engine, replace
with a snap and four clicks, sound
of the truck hood slamming shut,
everything beneath it a steady hum.

# What Becomes of Song

*anything dinged, busted or dumped / can be beaten till it*
*sings. / A kind of ghostly joy in it, / though this music's almost*
*unrecognizable, // so utterly of the coming world it is.*
—Mark Doty, "Tunnel Music"

Sense of sound sharpened, defense against
the cataract shroud grief gifts us with
till we can bear the light again.
I've listened hard these months,
sometimes for your off-key song,
sometimes the snap of twigs behind me
on our path beside the pond, so sure of it
I extend my hand behind me, expecting.

The song at first, right after the telling,
after the breath rushes back in,
is the moment after gunfire,
the violent break of air around you,
the ringing that carries a single pitch, monotone,
a hymn called out from the church front,
to an empty room, congregationless. And then,
somewhere from the buffeted landscape around you,
one by one, redwing calls and creaking trees,
then heat bugs and pond peepers, and you listen like epiphany
even if the call-and-answer isn't something you can
muster your own chords to return, and some point
before you realize it, you find your hand reaching
not behind you but in front, in supplication, in receipt
of all that sings and whirs and bears you back to what is familiar still
and what is still to come.

# Publications

My thanks to the editors of the following publications in which these poems first appeared, sometimes in slightly different form:

- *Appalachian Heritage*: "Cleave," "Hillbilly Transplant: Pondering Park Dominoes and the Death of Celia Cruz," "Passing of Grief," and "Hillbilly Transplant: Working at the Metropolitan Opera"

- *Cutleaf*: "Smoke, Salt, Sweet" and "Hillbilly Transplant: Seed and Scatter"

- *Drafthorse Literary Journal*: "Beautiful," "Deployment: Homefront," "Heaving," and "Tracer"

- *Heartwood Literary Magazine*: "Hillbilly Transplant Writes 'Where I'm From' Exercise with Imposter Narrative" and "Prevarication"

- *Kudzu*: "Thus Always to Tyrants" and "What Becomes of Sound"

- *Pine Mountain Sand & Gravel*: "Hillbilly Transplant: Seeing Child on Junction Boulevard Subway Platform," "Hillbilly Transplant: New Home," and "Republic/Church 2017-2020"

- *The Southern Poetry Anthology, Vol. IX: Virginia*: "Deployment: Homefront," "Hillbilly Transplant: Bethesda Fountain, Central Park," "Observations of Escape," and "What We Kill to Save" (Texas Review Press)

- *Still: The Journal*: "The Preacher's Daughter Studies Her Reflection"

- *Women of Appalachia Project: Women Speak, Vol 7*: "You Can't Leave It When You Go" and "Cannery in Seasons" (Sheila-Na-Gig Editions, 2021)

- *Women of Appalachia Project: Women Speak, Vol 8*: "Big K Radio: Snow Day," "Hillbilly Transplant: In 72nd Street Subway Tunnel a Meditation on Home," and "Under the Sugar Moon" (Sheila-Na-Gig Editions, 2022)

# Acknowledgments

I am grateful, always, for my amazing family who've been telling stories and singing around me for as long as I've had memories. I'm especially grateful for my sister Laura, my first and best friend. A particular gratitude for being able to be on "the compound" with my family during these pandemic years, to be there for family dinners, to relish the game nights and the laughter, and to get this book finished. Thank you to Jackson and Peyton whose company I adore and whose attention I'm so grateful for as they get older and still let me hang out with them. Thanks to my dad for all the things we've built together, for quiet days on the pond, and raucous nights playing cutthroat cards. Thanks to my mom for a lifetime of belly laughter and for setting an example of how to live fiercely with your heart and arms wide open. Thanks to Rae for laughing at everything we shouldn't have, and for sharing an appreciation for roadin with the windows down, and driving through a tornado for good catfish and fried okra.

My life has been especially blessed by amazing friends who've encouraged and supported me and my writing for years. For my Appalachian writing family, especially Jane Hicks, Silas House, and Darnell Arnoult, thank you for all the things, big and small, over the decades that have shaped my work and my life. Every summer night singing on porches at the Hindman Settlement School or in the breezeways at the Mountain Heritage Literary Festival provided the backdrop of my best creative memories. Every workshop getting to learn from Crystal Wilkinson, Aaron Smith, or Connie Green at LMU was a gift I'm so grateful for in the years I've spent pulling this book together. A considerable debt of gratitude to the Tennessee Mountain Writers for all the workshops on Orr Mountain, and to the amazing Bill Brown who is the most prolific poet and conscientious thinker I've ever had the pleasure to write with and call my friend. Thank you to Linda Parsons whose support and generous spirit made her the perfect editor for this book, and to Jesse Graves for plucking my manuscript out of the sea of amazing work. A huge thank you to the talented people at Madville for ushering this book into the world.

Special thanks to Elida Loya who has been my sister-friend, confidante, and my earliest battle buddy in so many ways, and to Jane Hicks who knows all the things and whose soul I recognized the day I met her. To my found family, you know who you are and I'm so glad we're on this ride together. My fierce girls, Nicole Hallingstad, Aminah Williams, Suzanne Meth, Alex Sare, Deb White, and Jo Bailey, are the kind of women I want to be if I ever grow up. Thanks to Maye Todd who's my biggest cheerleader outside our family and who has been asking for this book for years. A lifetime of love and gratitude to Myron and Nancy Stevenson for all their love and support, and especially for the way they serve, honor, and remember. A tremendous thank you to my Defense family, far too many to name here, who've made doing a really hard job a whole lot more fun these last two decades. My supreme thanks to my National Facilitator mentors, Myron Stevenson, Jim Holt, and Chris Jones, for all the lessons and shared moments; what a ride it was! Thanks to my amazing Stellar Solutions leadership who made a path for me to sit outside the wire for several months and catch my breath when I needed to; that tactical pause meant more than I can explain. Lastly, thank you to my military friends and families, for your friendship, love, and for all you bear—spoken and unspoken.

## About the Author

Lisa Parker is a native Virginian, a poet, musician, and photographer. Her first book, *This Gone Place*, won the 2010 ASA Weatherford Award, and her work is widely published in literary journals and anthologies. Her photography has been on exhibit in NYC and published in several arts journals and anthologies. She has worked in the Department of Defense for nearly 20 years, worked as a first responder for 15 years, and currently serves as a crisis and disaster response volunteer with Team Rubicon. Some of her work may be found at www.wheatpark.com.